EXPLORE THE MIDWEST

by Kristine Spanier, MLIS

Ideas for Parents and Teachers

Pogo Books let children practice reading informational text while introducing them to nonfiction features such as headings, labels, sidebars, maps, and diagrams, as well as a table of contents, glossary, and index.

Carefully leveled text with a strong photo match offers early fluent readers the support they need to succeed.

Before Reading

- "Walk" through the book and point out the various nonfiction features. Ask the student what purpose each feature serves.
- Look at the glossary together. Read and discuss the words.

Read the Book

- Have the child read the book independently.
- Invite him or her to list questions that arise from reading.

After Reading

- Discuss the child's questions. Talk about how he or she might find answers to those questions.
- Prompt the child to think more. Ask: Have you visited different regions of the United States? What did you see?

Pogo Books are published by Jump!
5357 Penn Avenue South
Minneapolis, MN 55419
www.jumplibrary.com

Library of Congress Cataloging-in-Publication Data

Names: Spanier, Kristine, author.
Title: Explore the Midwest / by Kristine Spanier, MLIS.
Description: Minneapolis, MN : Jump!, Inc., [2023]
Series: Regions of the United States
"Pogo Books." | Audience: Ages 7-10
Identifiers: LCCN 2021053215 (print)
LCCN 2021053216 (ebook)
ISBN 9781636907178 (hardcover)
ISBN 9781636907185 (paperback)
ISBN 9781636907192 (ebook)
Subjects: LCSH: Middle West–Juvenile literature.
Classification: LCC F351 .S734 2023 (print)
LCC F351 (ebook) | DDC 977–dc23/eng/20211106
LC record available at https://lccn.loc.gov/2021053215
LC ebook record available at https://lccn.loc.gov/2021053216

Editor: Jenna Gleisner
Designer: Molly Ballanger

Photo Credits: Zeljko Radojko/Shutterstock, cover (top); Songquan Deng/Shutterstock, cover (middle); Charles Knowles/Shutterstock, cover (bottom); William Gottemoller/Shutterstock, 1; Volodymyr Burdiak/Shutterstock, 3; Davel5957/iStock, 4; agefotostock/Alamy, 5; BrAt82/Shutterstock, 6-7 (background); North Wind Picture Archives/Alamy, 6-7 (map); Jacob Boomsma/Shutterstock, 8; Universal Images Group/SuperStock, 9; Martin Procházka/Dreamstime, 10-11tl; Jess Kraft/Shutterstock, 10-11tr; Lynn_Bystrom/iStock, 10-11bl; Jesse Nguyen/Shutterstock, 10-11br; RobertWaltman/iStock, 12-13; Jim Parkin/Shutterstock, 14-15; Felix Mizioznikov/Shutterstock, 16; UPI/Alamy, 17; Maksymowicz/iStock, 18-19; Valentin Valkov/Shutterstock, 20-21tl; Suzanne Tucker/Shutterstock, 20-21tr; JamesBrey/iStock, 20-21bl; Alexey Fedorenko/Shutterstock, 20-21br; Arlene Waller/Shutterstock, 22t; Sean Pavone/Shutterstock, 22m; Zack Frank/Shutterstock, 22b; Marti Bug Catcher/Shutterstock, 23.

Printed in the United States of America at Corporate Graphics in North Mankato, Minnesota.

Title Page Image: Apostle Islands, Lake Superior, Wisconsin

TABLE OF CONTENTS

CHAPTER 1

HISTORY AND LOCATION

This is the Gateway Arch in St. Louis, Missouri. It is sometimes called the Gateway to the West. Why? France once owned the land west of the Mississippi River. U.S. President Thomas Jefferson bought it in 1803. This was the Louisiana Purchase.

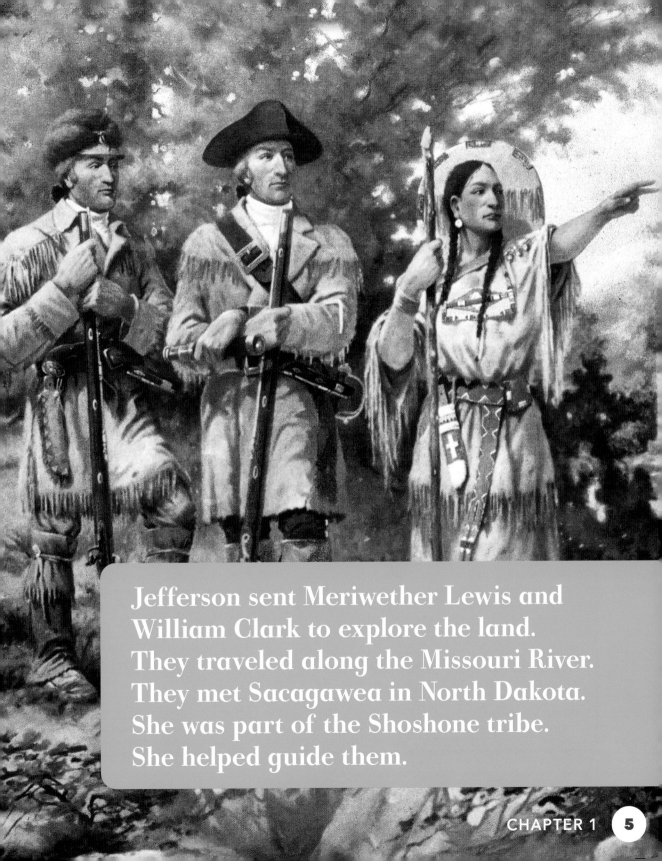

Jefferson sent Meriwether Lewis and William Clark to explore the land. They traveled along the Missouri River. They met Sacagawea in North Dakota. She was part of the Shoshone tribe. She helped guide them.

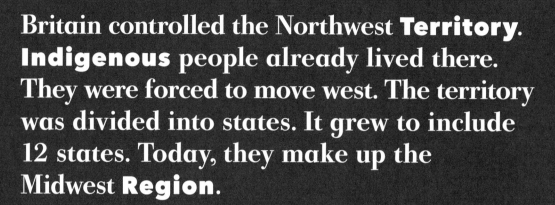

Britain controlled the Northwest **Territory**. **Indigenous** people already lived there. They were forced to move west. The territory was divided into states. It grew to include 12 states. Today, they make up the Midwest **Region**.

Northwest Territory

THE UNITED STATES in 1792

The Mississippi was then the western boundary of the United States, but we had a claim on the Oregon country. (See above). England, Spain and Russia also claimed Oregon.

SCALE OF MILES

0 50 100 200 300 400 500

TAKE A LOOK!

Which states are part of the Midwest? Take a look!

CHAPTER 2

GEOGRAPHY AND WILDLIFE

The Mississippi River is the second-longest river in the country. It runs through the Midwest. It begins in Minnesota. It ends in Louisiana.

HERE 1475 FT
ABOVE
THE OCEAN
THE MIGHTY
MISSISSIPPI
BEGINS
TO FLOW
ON ITS
WINDING WAY
2552 MILES
TO THE
GULF OF
MEXICO

Mississippi River Headwaters

Four of the five Great Lakes are in this region. Michigan borders all four. It is made of two **peninsulas**.

Michigan

northern pike

bison

black bear

cardinals

The Midwest has many lakes. They are filled with freshwater fish. Bison roam the plains. Black bears prowl the woods. Cardinals fly the skies.

Part of the Great Plains are in the Midwest. Prairie grasses grow.

DID YOU KNOW?

Part of the Midwest is known as **Tornado** Alley. Why? This area has more tornadoes than anywhere else in the world!

Great Plains

Black Hills

The Black Hills are in South Dakota. Pine trees cover the area. They look black from far away. This is how the mountains got their name.

WHAT DO YOU THINK?

Black Elk Peak is in the Black Hills. It is the tallest peak in the Midwest. It is 7,242 feet (2,207 meters) high. What **landforms** are near you?

CHAPTER 3

DAILY LIFE

Chicago, Illinois, is the Midwest's most **populated** city. It is the third most populated city in the United States. Navy Pier is here. It juts into Lake Michigan.

Navy Pier

Would you like to go to a football game? Ohio has two teams in the National Football League! The Pro Football Hall of Fame is here, too.

Many people here work in transportation and **manufacturing**. Michigan makes a lot of vehicles. Wisconsin is known for its cows. They provide the country with milk, butter, and cheese.

TAKE A LOOK!

What are some of the Midwest's top **industries**? Take a look!

Illinois

Indiana

Iowa
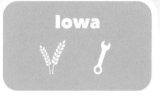

Kansas

Michigan

Minnesota

Missouri

Nebraska

North Dakota

Ohio

South Dakota

Wisconsin

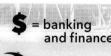 = banking and finance   = farming   = food processing   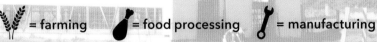 = manufacturing

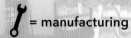 = mining   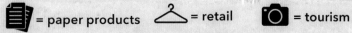 = paper products   = retail   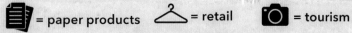 = tourism

spring crops

summer lake

fall harvest

winter ice fishing

The weather changes with every season. In spring, farmers plant **crops**. Lakes are nice to swim in during the hot summers. Fall is the time to **harvest**. Some people ice fish on frozen lakes in winter.

Do you want to spend time in the Midwest? What would you like to do first?

MIDWEST REGION

Location: north-central United States

Population (2021 estimate): 68,841,444

Most Populated City in Each State:
Chicago, IL
Indianapolis, IN
Des Moines, IA
Wichita, KS
Detroit, MI
Minneapolis, MN
Kansas City, MO
Omaha, NE
Fargo, ND
Columbus, OH
Sioux Falls, SD
Milwaukee, WI

Top Industries: farming, food processing, manufacturing, mining, paper production, tourism

Average High Temperature:
mid-80 degrees Fahrenheit (30 degrees Celsius)

Average Low Temperature:
15 degrees Fahrenheit (−9 degrees Celsius)

Major Landforms: Great Plains, Badlands, Sand Hills, Black Hills

Highest Point: Black Elk Peak, SD, 7,242 feet (2,207 m)

Major Waterways: Mississippi River, Missouri River, Arkansas River, Ohio River, Lake Superior, Lake Michigan, Lake Huron, Lake Erie

Major Landmarks: Chimney Rock, Crazy Horse Memorial, Gateway Arch, Navy Pier, Mount Rushmore

INDIANAPOLIS, IN

BADLANDS, SD

CHIMNEY ROCK, NE

crops: Plants grown for food.

harvest: The gathering of crops that are ready to eat.

Indigenous: Of or relating to the earliest known people to live in a place.

industries: Businesses or trades.

landforms: Natural features of land surfaces.

manufacturing: The industry of making something on a large scale using special equipment or machinery.

peninsulas: Pieces of land that stick out from a larger landmass and are almost completely surrounded by water.

populated: Having people living in it.

region: A general area or a specific district or territory.

territory: The land under the control of a state, nation, or ruler.

tornado: A violent and very destructive windstorm that appears as a dark cloud shaped like a funnel.

Mount Rushmore, South Dakota

INDEX

TO LEARN MORE

Finding more information is as easy as 1, 2, 3.

1. Go to www.factsurfer.com
2. Enter "exploretheMidwest" into the search box.
3. Choose your book to see a list of websites.

FACT SURFER